MEAL PLANNER

SHAY SHULL

HARVEST HOUSE PUBLISHERS
EUGENE, OREGON

Mix-and-Match Meal Planner

Copyright © 2016 Mix and Match Mama
Published by Harvest House Publishers
Eugene, Oregon 97402
www.harvesthousepublishers.com

978-0-7369-6611-5
Cover and interior design by Faceout Studio
Cover photos © B. and E. Dudzinscy, Brent Hofacker, Bhakpong, Rustle, Joshua Resnick / Shutterstock
Published in association with William K. Jensen Literary Agency, 119 Bampton Court, Eugene, Oregon 97404.

Printed in China

15 16 17 18 19 20 21 22 23 / DS-FO / 10 9 8 7 6 5 4 3 2 1

To Mom—

You never meal-planned
but always managed to
deliver a spectacular supper.

xo

CONTENTS

INTRODUCTION

What's for dinner? That famous phrase that can make a woman's heart beat just a little faster. What's for dinner? What's for dinner? What *is* for dinner? Hmmm...

Growing up, my mom put a hot meal on the table each and every night. It was always home-made, it was always delicious, and it was always spur-of-the-moment. My mom is famous for being in the middle of actually cooking our dinner (like ground beef was browning) and yet still not knowing what we were going to be having—a mere 15 minutes later! That is how my mom meal-planned. As she was cooking, she was planning.

Me? I need a very specific meal plan for the week. I need exact recipes, a solid grocery list, a well-stocked pantry, and a plan. I like to prepare everything in advance so that on busy weeknights, I know exactly what to reach for and exactly what to prepare. I need a meal plan.

Two years ago on my blog, I introduced Meal-Planning Mondays to my readers and the feedback was very positive. Apparently, every-one wants help meal planning. From single gals to newlyweds, from busy moms with small kids to retired couples, everyone agreed: Cooking isn't hard; it's deciding what to make that can be challenging.

Each week, I started giving my readers five simple suppers plus a sweet treat or two for their week. Nothing complicated, nothing time consuming—just good, solid dinner recipes to help busy women get supper on the table. My meal plans change by the season and they never have lengthy ingredient lists, uncommon spices, or take a long time to prepare. They're perfect weeknight meals.

Unless noted, all entree recipes in this book serve four.

Mix & Match

METHOD

When my friends and I were new moms, our friend Rachel began serving everyone this delicious Chocolate Chip Bundt Cake. We loved this cake so much that everyone I knew asked for the recipe and began making it for their special events, cozy dinners, potluck suppers, and showers galore. This cake was everywhere. About a year later, I just couldn't make the same cake any more, but I didn't want to make another kind because I knew that the tried-and-true Chocolate Chip Bundt Cake was always easy, always moist, always turned out, and always a crowd pleaser...so I decided to mix and match it. I took Rachel's basic method and made a butterscotch cake instead. Same fabulous results but with an entirely new flavor and presentation. The next time, I made a lemon version, then a pumpkin version, and then about 10 versions later, Rachel asked me how many I thought I could make, and I said probably 100. Well, 101 Bundt cakes later I proved to myself that sometimes the best things on the table are just basic recipes with a little twist. I find that most women aren't looking for fancy and complicated...we're looking for tried-and-true. I applied this mix-and-match concept to everything I made and voilà! Instead of Sloppy Joes, we had Buffalo Turkey Joes. Instead of burgers, we had Pizza Burgers. Instead of tacos, we had Sweet-and-Sour Chicken Tacos, and so on. Everyday suppers are a lot more fun when you start mixing and matching. And the best part? They're still the same basic methods you rely on for your busy weeknights...just with a twist.

SLOW COOKER TIPS

Other than my coffeepot, the most-used small appliance in my house is the slow cooker. I used to be one of those people who only pulled my slow cooker out during the fall and winter, but I've learned the slow cooker is actually a perfect year-round tool. It is such a time saver for busy families! Trust me, with a few of these tips you'll be rethinking that old slow cooker too.

1. Buy a slow cooker that is oval, not round. You need one that will fit longer cuts of meats (like roasts and briskets) and long spaghetti noodles. Round slow cookers just aren't as functional. To me, a 6- to 7-quart slow cooker is ideal for dinners.

2. Buy a slow cooker with a high, low, and warm setting. You'll be amazed at how much use you can get out of a slow cooker with all three settings. Sometimes you have all day to cook, sometimes just a few hours, and sometimes you just need to keep your food warm until serving.

3. For dips and small appetizers, use a small slow cooker. Your slow cooker needs to be at least half full before using it, and a dip won't take up that much space.

4. Slow cooker liners can make cleanup a breeze. These handy little liners are found on the foil and baggie aisle and are placed inside your slow cooker before you add your food. After you're done eating, just toss the bag in the trash and cleanup is over. Such a simple little step really helps out.

5. Always brown your beef before placing it in the slow cooker (yes, Mom, I'm talking to you!). Browning your meat beforehand adds so much more flavor and depth to the entire dish. It just takes a few minutes because you're not cooking it all the way through—you're just browning it! Chicken breasts do not require cooking beforehand but any ground meat (beef, chicken or turkey) or large roast or brisket does.

6. Add something fresh to your slow cooker meal when you're done. I always add some fresh herbs, chopped green onions, cheese, or sour cream to the top. Just a little something fresh wakens the dish up and gives the whole slow cooker meal an extra oomph!

Whether you have a big family or small, single or not, you should invest in a slow cooker. Nothing is better (especially during the cold days of fall and winter) than coming home and smelling your yummy supper already bubbling away.

PERFECT CHICKEN

If I'm preparing dinner for my family on a weeknight, I don't have time to boil and poach chicken, let it cool a bit, shred it, and then use it in the recipe. That is way too many steps. When I'm ready to start making dinner, I want to jump straight to the recipe with my shredded chicken ready and waiting on me. How do I solve this problem? I let my chicken cook all day in the slow cooker and then jump right into the recipe when I get home.

It's so simple! All you do is put your uncooked chicken in the slow cooker with just enough water to cover it, set the temp on low, and let it cook for 6 to 8 hours. (If you're using frozen chicken, let it cook 8 hours.) You can also place the heat on high and cook 3 to 4 hours.

When you get home from your busy day, you just remove the cooked chicken from the slow cooker and it will shred right up with two forks. It's always moist and always ready to be used in a variety of dishes.

You can cook your chicken all day in just water or you can use some chicken stock, salsa, Sprite, BBQ sauce, marinara sauce, a package of taco seasoning, a package of dry Ranch dressing mix...Go nuts! Whatever you flavor your chicken with will add more flavor to your final dish. Simple.

Never fuss with chicken again. Place it in the slow cooker, set your temp, and leave it alone. The perfect chicken will be waiting when you're ready to start cooking.

PANTRY ESSENTIALS

SEASONINGS

chili powder

salt

pepper

Worcestershire sauce

cumin

taco seasoning

red pepper flakes

oregano

Italian seasoning

BAKING SUPPLIES

vanilla

baking soda

sugar

flour

CONDIMENTS

ketchup

mustard

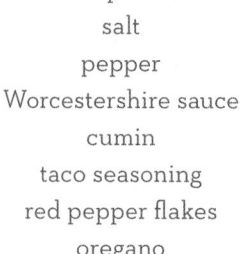

OILS

butter

extra virgin olive oil

vegetable oil

cooking spray

YEAR-AT-A-GLANCE

SPRING WEEK ONE
Tex-Mex Chicken Pot Pie
Spring Vegetable Risotto
Hawaiian BBQ Chicken Burritos
Sausage and Leek Pasta
Pesto Meatballs
Lemon Blueberry Cream Pie

SUMMER WEEK ONE
Tomatillo and Pineapple Burgers
Spicy Shrimp Pasta
Greek Tacos
Enchilada Suizas
Buffalo Chicken Paninis
Hawaiian Luau Bundt Cake

SPRING WEEK TWO
Spicy Chicken Baked Tacos
Mushroom Sausage Kale Pasta
Coconut-Crusted Chicken
Cheeseburger Meatballs
Chicken Florentine Enchiladas
Strawberry Shortcake Trifle

SUMMER WEEK TWO
BLT Pasta
Ranch Burgers with Avocado Ranch Sauce
Grilled Shrimp Tacos
Spinach and Sundried Tomato Joes
Chicken Chili Verde
Key Lime Pie Bars

FALL WEEK ONE
BBQ Apple Chicken Sandwiches
Sweet Potato Shepherd's Pie
Mexican Minestrone
Crunchy BBQ Brisket Tacos
Sausage and Broccoli Tortellini Bake
Pumpkin Spice Cupcakes

WINTER WEEK ONE
Beef Enchiladas
Spaghetti and Meat Sauce
Italian Brisket Sandwiches
Spinach and Chicken Noodle Soup
Beer Chicken Chili
Cherry Berry Cobbler

FALL WEEK TWO
Enchilada Chili
Chicken à la King
Brown Sugar Brisket
Sausage and Butternut Squash Pasta
Pizza Meatballs
Caramel Apple Bread Pudding

WINTER WEEK TWO
Mom's Meatloaf
Creamy Tomato Chicken Pasta
Beefy Cornbread Casserole
Pepperoni Pizza Soup
Chicken Citrus Tostadas
Butterfinger Blondies

SPRING

WEEK ONE MENU

MONDAY	Tex-Mex Chicken Pot Pie
TUESDAY	Spring Vegetable Risotto
WEDNESDAY	Hawaiian BBQ Chicken Burritos
THURSDAY	Sausage and Leek Pasta
FRIDAY	Pesto Meatballs
SOMETHING SWEET	Lemon Blueberry Cream Pie

WEEK TWO MENU

MONDAY · Spicy Chicken Baked Tacos

TUESDAY · Mushroom Sausage Kale Pasta

WEDNESDAY · Coconut-Crusted Chicken

THURSDAY · Cheeseburger Meatballs

FRIDAY · Chicken Florentine Enchiladas

SOMETHING SWEET · Strawberry Shortcake Trifle

WEEK 1 SHOPPING LIST

PRODUCE

2 small onions
1 green bell pepper
2 jalapeno peppers
8-10 green onions
2 zucchini
10 asparagus stalks
9-12 cloves garlic
3 leeks
8-10 basil leaves
1 pint fresh blueberries
½ cup lemon juice

MEATS

3 lbs. chicken
1 lb. ground beef
1 lb. bulk Italian sausage
(hot or sweet)

CANNED FOODS, CONDIMENTS, SOUPS, SAUCES

1 10-oz. can Rotel tomatoes
1 6-oz. can tomato paste
72 oz. chicken stock
12 oz. chicken broth (1½ cups)
1 cup BBQ sauce

CANNED FOODS, CONDIMENTS, SOUPS, SAUCES (CONT'D)

1 8-oz. can crushed pineapple
1 8-oz. jar sundried tomatoes in oil
4 oz. premade pesto (1/2 cup)
spaghetti sauce (optional for garnish)

GRAINS, PASTA, BREAD

1 cup Arborio rice
5 burrito-sized tortillas
1 lb. pasta (we use whole wheat rotini)
1 can refrigerated biscuits

FROZEN

1 cup frozen corn
1 cup frozen peas
1 box frozen spinach

BAKING

1 cup Panko (or other breadcrumbs)
1 14-oz. can sweetened condensed milk
1/4 cup powdered sugar
1 3-oz. package lemon instant pudding mix
1 premade graham cracker crust
2 tablespoons blueberry preserves or jam

DAIRY

1 cup shredded Cheddar cheese
1 1/2 cups Parmesan cheese
1 8-oz. package cream cheese
2 eggs
2 splashes milk
whipped cream

** Don't forget to stock up on your Pantry Essentials
(see page 14)

TEX-MEX CHICKEN POT PIE

MON

Really, *is there anything more comforting* than Chicken Pot Pie? I think not. I decided to *mix and match* it and make a Tex-Mex version. Yummy!

INGREDIENTS

- 1 lb. chopped, cooked chicken
  (see how I do it on page 12)
- 1 small onion, chopped
- 1 green bell pepper, chopped
- 1 jalapeno pepper, seeded and chopped
  (optional)
- 1 10-oz. can Rotel tomatoes (do not drain)
- 1 6-oz. can tomato paste

- 1 tablespoon chili powder
- 1 cup chicken stock
- 1 cup frozen corn
- 1 can refrigerated biscuits
- salt and pepper
- 1 cup Cheddar cheese, shredded

Preheat oven to 425°. Lightly spray an 8 x 8-inch baking dish with cooking spray; set aside. In a large skillet, combine the cooked chicken, onion, bell pepper, jalapeno pepper, Rotel, tomato paste, chili powder, stock, and corn over medium-high heat. Add in a pinch of salt and pepper and bring to simmer for about five minutes.

After simmering, pour the chicken mixture into your prepared baking dish. Remove biscuits from the can and lay them across the top of mixture in the baking dish. Sprinkle a little cheese over the tops of each biscuit.

Bake for 8-10 minutes or until biscuits are brown and chicken mixture is bubbly. Remove from oven and serve. Everyone gets a scoop of Tex-Mex filling with a cheesy biscuit on top!

SPRING VEGETABLE RISOTTO

Now that it's spring, the *food needs to be fresh, light, and simple.* This would be a nice side dish with a piece of fish or steak, and it makes a great vegetarian dinner too. However, I love chicken in the risotto. You can buy a rotisserie chicken from the grocery store and shred that right in, use leftover chicken from a previous supper, bake some chicken in the oven, or use my Perfect Chicken method (see instructions on page 12).

INGREDIENTS

- 2 quarts chicken stock (or veggie stock if you're making this a vegetarian dish)
- 1 tablespoon butter
- 1 tablespoon extra virgin olive oil
- 2 zucchini, chopped
- 10 asparagus stalks, chopped
- 1 onion, chopped
- 3-6 cloves garlic, chopped
- 1 cup Arborio rice
- 1 cup frozen peas
- 2 cups chopped, cooked chicken (optional)
- $\frac{1}{2}$ cup Parmesan cheese, grated
- salt and pepper

In a large stock pot, bring chicken stock up to low simmer (not boiling). In a separate pan, melt butter with 1 tablespoon olive oil over medium-high heat. Add in zucchini and asparagus and sauté 4-5 minutes. Remove veggies from pan, cover, and set aside. Add onion and garlic to skillet and cook 4-5 minutes. Stir in rice for another minute.

At this point, take a ladle and add 1 cup of your hot stock to the rice. Stir constantly for a minute or so. As the liquid evaporates, the rice will become super starchy and delicious. Stir pretty often, adding stock every time the majority of the liquid evaporates. You will continue doing this for about 18 minutes. Add stock, stir, wait for it to evaporate, and add more. This will cause the risotto to fluff up and look creamy (without using any cream!) A lot of recipes will tell you to stir continuously, but you don't need to. Just stir it around every few minutes and you'll be fine.

After the rice is tender (take a bite!), stir in frozen peas, zucchini, asparagus, and chicken and continue cooking another 3-4 minutes. Stir in cheese; season with lots of salt and pepper to taste.

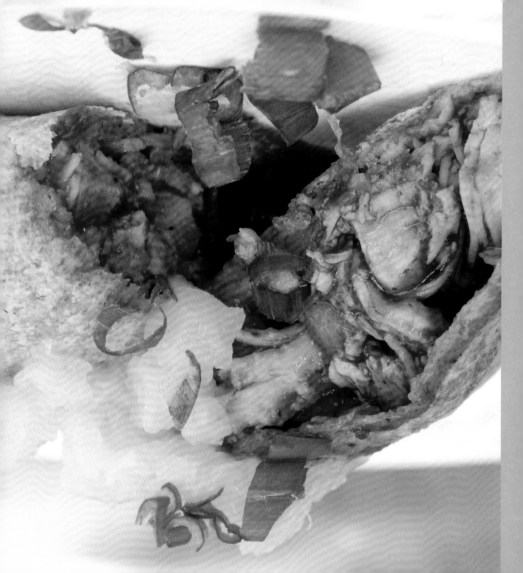

HAWAIIAN BBQ CHICKEN BURRITOS

I'm really into the *sweet and spicy flavors for spring*. This little twist on a burrito takes the sweetness of pineapple and matches it with the spiciness of jalapeno. If you're serving your kiddos, you can just use a little less jalapeno. This is totally kid-friendly!

INGREDIENTS

1 lb. cooked, shredded chicken
(see how I get it on page 12)
1 cup BBQ sauce
1 jalapeno pepper, seeds removed and chopped
(use less if you want less heat!)
1 8-oz. can crushed pineapple
8-10 green onions, chopped
5 burrito-sized tortillas

Preheat your oven to 375°. In a mixing bowl, combine chicken, BBQ sauce, jalapeno pepper, pineapple, and green onions. Spoon chicken mixture down the center of each of your tortillas. Roll the tortillas burrito style by folding the ends down and then folding over each side.

Place the burritos seam side down on a foil lined baking sheet that has been lightly greased. Bake 15-18 minutes or until lightly browned. You can drizzle a little extra pineapple, BBQ sauce, and/or green onions over each one before you serve.

SAUSAGE AND LEEK PASTA

Leeks make me happy. They're the perfect little sister to the onion and they just make me happy. They're mild and so versatile, especially in a pasta dish. We used a bulk Italian pork sausage in this meal but you can certainly substitute a chicken or turkey sausage.

INGREDIENTS

1 lb. pasta (we use whole wheat rotini)
1 lb. bulk Italian sausage, either hot or sweet
3 leeks, washed (see below) and chopped
3 cloves garlic, chopped
1½ cups chicken broth
1 8-oz. jar sundried tomatoes in oil, drained

½ cup Parmesan cheese, grated
8-10 basil leaves, torn or chopped
extra virgin olive oil
salt and pepper

Bring a large pot of water to boil, drop pasta in, and cook until al dente (7-8 minutes).

Meanwhile, over medium-high heat, heat a couple of tablespoons of olive oil in a large pan. Once hot, add in sausage to brown (about 6 minutes). Let it brown without stirring it too often; drain. Add in leeks and garlic and sauté another 5 minutes. Add in chicken stock and lots of salt and pepper. Scrape up the little bits off the bottom of the pan, lower the heat to medium-low, and simmer 3-5 minutes. Stir in sun-dried tomatoes.

Drain pasta and add to sausage mixture. Stir in cheese and basil.

Note: Leeks are grown in sandy soil, so you can't just wash the outsides; you have to wash the insides too. The easiest way is to chop the leeks, place them in a colander in your sink, and then run lots of cold water over the tops. Use a paper towel to lightly pat them dry.

PESTO MEATBALLS

Meatball night is a big deal at my house. The kids love the taste and I love hiding all sorts of veggies inside. You could prepare this as an appetizer, with pasta, or with a big side salad. My pound of ground beef produced 10 large meatballs, but the size is up to you. You can also use ground turkey instead of beef in this recipe.

INGREDIENTS

1 lb. ground beef
3 cloves garlic, chopped
1 cup Panko (or other breadcrumbs of your choice)
$\frac{1}{2}$ cup Parmesan cheese, grated
1 box frozen spinach, defrosted and excess
   water squeezed out
$\frac{1}{2}$ cup pesto (store-bought or homemade)
2 eggs, beaten

2 splashes milk
salt and pepper
1-2 tablespoons extra virgin olive oil
spaghetti sauce for dipping or drizzling
   on top (optional)

Preheat oven to 425°. In a medium bowl, combine ground beef, garlic, Panko, cheese, spinach, pesto, eggs, and milk. Add in just a pinch of salt and pepper. Roll into balls and place on a lightly greased baking sheet (I always line mine with foil for easy clean up!). Drizzle olive oil over all of the meatballs. Roast in the oven about 20 minutes or until brown.

LEMON BLUEBERRY CREAM PIE

My cousin Brooke gave me this recipe and it is the perfect dessert to make with kids. *No oven, no knives, just yummy goodness.*

INGREDIENTS

1 8-oz. package cream cheese, softened
1 14-oz. can sweetened condensed milk
$1/4$ cup powdered sugar
1 3-oz. package lemon instant pudding mix
  (do not prepare—you just need the powder)
2 teaspoons lemon zest

$1/2$ cup fresh lemon juice
1 premade graham cracker crust
1 pint fresh blueberries
2 tablespoons blueberry preserves or jam
whipped cream to garnish

In a large mixing bowl, beat cream cheese, milk, and powdered sugar with an electric mixer until creamy. Beat in lemon pudding mix, lemon zest, and lemon juice until just blended. Pour half of lemon mixture into your prepared pie crust.

Stir together fresh blueberries with blueberry preserves in a small bowl. Pour the blueberry mixture evenly over the top of the lemon pie layer. Top the blueberry layer with the other half of your lemon mixture. Chill pie at least two hours (you can even chill it overnight!). Remove pie from fridge and cut into wedges. Serve with a garnish of whipped cream.

WEEK 2 SHOPPING LIST

PRODUCE

1 jalapeno pepper
1 shallot
2 cups mushrooms
4 cups kale
1 onion
1 red bell pepper
1 red onion
1 pint fresh strawberries

CANNED FOODS, CONDIMENTS, SOUPS, SAUCES

1 pkg. taco seasoning
1 cup chicken stock
relish to garnish
1 can cream of chicken soup
1 10-oz. can enchilada sauce
2 cups salsa
orange marmalade (garnish)

MEATS

3 lbs. chicken breast
1 lb. ground beef
1 lb. Italian sausage
(turkey, chicken, or pork)

GRAINS, PASTA, BREAD

6 to 8 taco shells
1 lb. pasta (we used penne)
8 tortillas (either flour or whole wheat)

BAKING

¾ cup Bisquick mix
1½ cups shredded sweetened coconut
½ cup breadcrumbs or Panko
1 5-oz. pkg. instant vanilla pudding
1 14-oz. can sweetened condensed milk
1 pound cake

FROZEN

2 boxes frozen spinach
1 12-oz. tub Cool Whip, thawed

DAIRY

2 cups Pepper Jack cheese
1 cup Parmesan cheese
1 cup Cheddar cheese
1 cup Monterey Jack cheese
3 eggs
3 cups milk
splash of half and half, whipping cream, or milk

** Don't forget to stock up on your Pantry Essentials
(see page 14)

SPICY CHICKEN BAKED TACOS

Simple and delicious—perfect for a busy weeknight! *You should totally try it. Tonight.*

INGREDIENTS

1 lb. cooked, shredded chicken breast
(see how I get it on page 12)

1 jalapeno pepper, chopped (remove the seeds
for less heat)

1 package taco seasoning

1 box frozen spinach, defrosted and excess
water squeezed out

2 cups salsa

extra virgin olive oil

6-8 taco shells

2 cups shredded Pepper Jack cheese

Preheat oven to 425°. In a large skillet over medium-high heat, combine cooked chicken, jalapeno pepper, taco seasoning, spinach, and salsa in a tablespoon or so of olive oil. Reduce the heat to low and simmer about 5 minutes.

Meanwhile, in an 8 x 8-inch baking dish sprayed with cooking spray, line up taco shells. Divide the chicken mixture between the shells. Top tacos with cheese and pop dish in the oven. Bake about 10 minutes or until the cheese is bubbly and brown.

MUSHROOM SAUSAGE KALE PASTA

My family loves pasta for supper, and I love making pasta like this for my kiddos because *they eat it up...kale and all.* If you're not into kale, feel free to substitute fresh spinach instead. Just *mix and match* it for your family!

INGREDIENTS

1 lb. Italian sausage (turkey, chicken, or pork)
1 lb. pasta (we used penne)
1 shallot, chopped
2 cups chopped mushrooms (any variety you like)
4 cups kale, torn into bite-sized pieces (just a few big handfuls)

1 cup chicken stock
1 cup Parmesan cheese, grated
splash of half and half, whipping cream, or milk
salt and pepper
extra virgin olive oil

In a large skillet over medium-high heat, drizzle in just a tablespoon or so of olive oil. Add sausage (if it's in the casing, remove from casing first) and begin to brown.

On a second burner, bring a large pot of water to boil for your pasta. Drop in pasta and cook to al dente.

Once your sausage is browned and crumbly, drain off fat and then add in chopped shallot and sauté just a minute or so. Add in chopped mushrooms and kale. Stir in your stock and deglaze the pan (scrape up the little bits off of the bottom of your pan). Reduce heat to medium and allow mixture to bubble up a few minutes.

Drain pasta and add to your sausage mixture. Stir in Parmesan cheese and a splash of half and half. Add just a pinch of salt and pepper and serve (maybe with a bit more Parmesan to garnish).

COCONUT-CRUSTED CHICKEN

Spooning *a little marmalade* over the top *takes things to a whole new level.* Serve it with green beans for a quick and easy weeknight meal!

INGREDIENTS

³/₄ cup Bisquick mix
1¹/₂ cups shredded sweetened coconut
pinch salt and pepper
1 egg, beaten

1 lb. chicken breasts
2 tablespoons butter, melted
orange marmalade for garnishing

Preheat oven to 400°. In one shallow dish (such as a pie plate), combine Bisquick, shredded coconut, and a pinch of salt and pepper. In a second shallow dish, beat the egg. Dip each chicken breast first in the beaten egg, coating well on both sides, and then in the Bisquick mixture.

Place chicken on greased, foil-lined baking sheet. Brush half the melted butter over the tops of the chicken and bake 8 minutes. Flip chicken over and brush remaining half of your melted butter on opposite side and cook another 8 minutes. Your chicken should be brown and crispy with the juices running clear. Remove chicken from oven and garnish with a little orange marmalade on top.

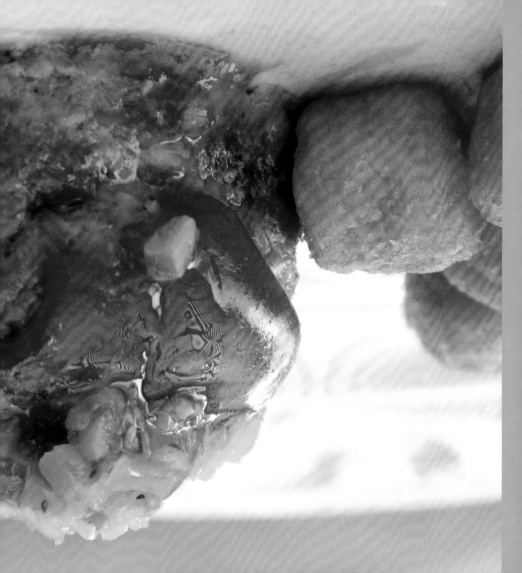

CHEESEBURGER MEATBALLS

THU

You guys know I'm meatball obsessed. Well, *I'm also cheeseburger obsessed.* So I turned meatballs into cheeseburgers. All the flavor but without the grill!

INGREDIENTS

1 lb. ground beef
1/2 cup breadcrumbs or Panko
1 cup Cheddar cheese, shredded
2 eggs, beaten
1 onion, finely chopped

generous pinches salt and pepper
4 tablespoons Worcestershire sauce, divided
1 1/2 cups ketchup
2 teaspoons mustard
relish to garnish

Preheat oven to 425°. Mix ground beef, breadcrumbs, cheese, eggs, onion, salt, pepper, and 2 tablespoons Worcestershire sauce in a bowl. Form into meatballs and line them up on a greased, foil-lined baking sheet.

Next, combine remaining 2 tablespoons Worcestershire sauce, ketchup, and mustard in a bowl. Top each meatball with sauce and bake 15-18 minutes, or until they're browned and cooked through. Garnish with a little relish.

CHICKEN FLORENTINE ENCHILADAS

We love making enchiladas at our house. They always look a little fancy, but they're a really simple weeknight supper. Honestly, this yummy meal can be on your table in less than 30 minutes. *From my table to yours, enjoy!*

INGREDIENTS

- 1 lb. cooked, shredded chicken (see how I get it on page 12)
- 1 box frozen spinach, thawed and excess water squeezed out
- 1 red bell pepper, chopped
- 1 red onion, chopped

- 1 can cream of chicken soup
- 2 teaspoons cumin (use chili powder if you don't have cumin)
- salt and pepper
- 1 cup Monterey Jack cheese, shredded
- 8 tortillas (either flour or whole wheat)
- 1 10-oz. can enchilada sauce

Preheat oven to 400°. Lightly spray an 8 x 8-inch baking dish with cooking spray; set aside. In a large mixing bowl, combine shredded chicken with spinach, bell pepper, half of the onion, cream of chicken soup, cumin, a pinch of salt and pepper, and cheese. Once combined, spread a little bit down the center of each tortilla. Roll and place in the prepared baking dish. Once all 8 enchiladas are tucked inside the baking dish, pour enchilada sauce on top of them.

Bake uncovered about 20 minutes or until the edges of the tortillas are lightly brown and everything is bubbling. Remove from oven and sprinkle the remaining red onion over the top.

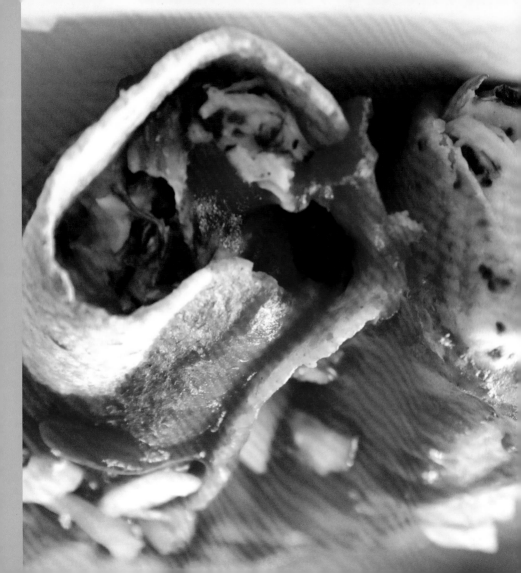

STRAWBERRY SHORTCAKE TRIFLE

This dessert should be made in advance. I make mine the day before and then wait 24 hours to serve. It's one of my favorites because it's *easy, easy, easy and yummy, yummy, yummy.* Trust me, your friends and family will love you for making this!

INGREDIENTS

1 5-oz. package instant vanilla pudding
3 cups milk
1 14-oz. can sweetened condensed milk
1 12-oz. tub Cool Whip, thawed
1 pound cake, cubed
1 pint fresh strawberries, sliced

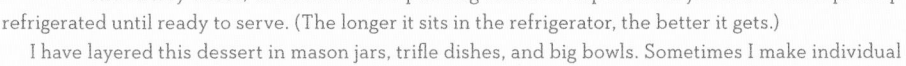

In a mixing bowl, combine pudding and milk with a whisk. Then whisk in sweetened condensed milk and Cool Whip. In your serving dish, layer some pound cake pieces, a few strawberry slices, and some of the pudding mixture. Repeat until you reach the top. Keep refrigerated until ready to serve. (The longer it sits in the refrigerator, the better it gets.)

I have layered this dessert in mason jars, trifle dishes, and big bowls. Sometimes I make individual trifles and sometimes I make one big dessert in a trifle dish. It's up to you!

FAMILY FAVORITES

MIX AND MATCH IDEAS

SUMMER

WEEK ONE MENU

MONDAY	Tomatillo and Pineapple Burgers
TUESDAY	Spicy Shrimp Pasta
WEDNESDAY	Greek Tacos
THURSDAY	Enchilada Suizas
FRIDAY	Buffalo Chicken Paninis
SOMETHING SWEET	Hawaiian Luau Bundt Cake

WEEK TWO MENU

MONDAY	BLT Pasta
TUESDAY	Ranch Burgers with Avocado Ranch Sauce
WEDNESDAY	Grilled Shrimp Tacos
THURSDAY	Spinach and Sundried Tomato Joes
FRIDAY	Chicken Chili Verde
SOMETHING SWEET	Key Lime Pie Bars

WEEK 1 SHOPPING LIST

PRODUCE

8-10 tomatillos

3-4 garlic cloves

2 onions

1 red onion

1 jalapeno pepper

1 lime

1 avocado

1 red bell pepper

4 cups fresh spinach

1 small cucumber

$\frac{1}{2}$ cup cherry tomatoes

chopped green onion (garnish)

MEATS

$1\frac{1}{2}$ lbs. ground beef

1 lb. frozen cooked and deveined shrimp

1 lb. ground turkey

1 lb. chicken

1 lb. grilled chicken

CANNED FOODS, CONDIMENTS, SOUPS, SAUCES

2 tablespoons steak seasoning

1 8-oz. can pineapple tidbits or crushed pineapple

1 15-oz. can crushed pineapple

1 cup chicken stock

chopped olives (optional)

CANNED FOODS, CONDIMENTS, SOUPS, SAUCES
(CONT'D)

1 can cream of mushroom soup

1 4-oz. can chopped green chilies

1 15-oz. can tomatillo or green chili enchilada sauce

½ cup of your favorite Buffalo hot sauce

6 tablespoons hummus

GRAINS, PASTA, BREAD

burger buns

1 lb. angel hair pasta

6 crunchy taco shells

8 tortillas

1 loaf bakery bread

BAKING

1 box coconut cake mix

2 small boxes instant coconut pudding (use vanilla if you can't find it)

1 container cream cheese frosting

2 cups sweetened, flaked coconut

Maraschino cherries (optional)

FROZEN

1 10-oz. box frozen spinach

DAIRY

4 slices Pepper Jack cheese

½ cup fresh feta cheese

1 cup Swiss cheese (plus a little extra for garnish)

½ cup Pepper Jack cheese, shredded

bleu cheese crumbles

4 eggs

** Don't forget to stock up on your Pantry Essentials (see page 14)

TOMATILLO AND PINEAPPLE BURGERS

MON

Burgers are a summertime necessity—but they don't have to be boring burgers! I've used home-made salsa in this recipe, but if you want to go the simple route, go ahead and use store-bought tomatillo salsa. Either way, you're going to love the flavor combination! *The sweetness of the pineapple* really pairs well *with the spiciness of the jalapeno pepper* and cheese.

INGREDIENTS

1½ lbs. ground beef
2 tablespoons steak seasoning
8-10 tomatillos, husks removed and rinsed off
3-4 garlic cloves
1 onion, sliced
1 jalapeno pepper, sliced (remove seeds for a
  less spicy version)
juice of one lime

1 8-oz. can pineapple tidbits or crushed
  pineapple, drained
1 avocado, sliced
4 slices pepper jack cheese
salt and pepper
burger buns

To make the salsa, combine tomatillos, garlic, onion, jalapeno pepper, and lime juice in the bowl of your food processor. Pulse until it reaches desired consistency. Stir in pineapple. Refrigerate until ready to eat. (For a simpler version, stir pineapple into store-bought tomatillo salsa.)

Preheat outdoor grill or indoor grill pan to medium-high. In a mixing bowl, combine ground beef with steak seasoning and a little salt and pepper. Divide ground beef mixture into 4 burger patties. Grill about 6 minutes each side. Add a slice of cheese on top about a minute before they're done.

To assemble your burgers, take one bun and top with burger patty, sliced avocado, and tomatillo-pineapple salsa. Serve open faced.

SPICY SHRIMP PASTA

I love shrimp. It's so versatile, easy to work with, and quick-cooking. All things I am looking for when making supper for my family. *This dish comes together in minutes.* I make ours spicy, but you can tame it to suit your family's tastes.

INGREDIENTS

1 lb. angel hair pasta
1 onion, chopped
1 red bell pepper, chopped
extra virgin olive oil
salt and pepper

1 lb. cooked and deveined frozen shrimp, thawed per package directions
1½ teaspoons red pepper flakes (use less for mild)
1 cup chicken stock
2 cups fresh spinach

Drop your pasta in a pot of boiling water and cook to al dente (about 5 minutes). Meanwhile, in a big skillet over medium-high heat, sauté your chopped onion and bell pepper in a drizzle of olive oil with a pinch of salt and pepper. Cook about 5 minutes.

Next, add in your shrimp and red pepper flakes and cook about a minute. Pour in your chicken stock and deglaze the pan (scrape the little bits off the bottom). Reduce heat to low.

Drain pasta and add to skillet. Stir to incorporate pasta with the other ingredients. Stir in fresh spinach and let it wilt down about a minute.

So fast, right? The angel hair pasta cooks up in minutes and the shrimp is already cooked, so all you're doing is heating it through.

GREEK TACOS

Grab some turkey, a little *hummus, fresh veggies, and feta* and make your own Greek tacos tonight.

INGREDIENTS

6 crunchy taco shells
1 lb. ground turkey
1 teaspoon oregano
1 10-oz. box frozen spinach, thawed and excess
   water squeezed out
6 tablespoons hummus, divided
1 red onion, chopped

1 small cucumber, chopped
$\frac{1}{2}$ cup cherry tomatoes, halved
chopped olives, optional
$\frac{1}{2}$ cup fresh feta cheese, crumbled
extra virgin olive oil
salt and pepper

Preheat oven to 350°. Place the taco shells on a baking sheet and lightly toast them for about 4 minutes; they burn quickly, so keep an eye on them. Remove from oven and set aside.

Meanwhile, in a large skillet over medium-high heat, drizzle in a tablespoon of olive oil and add the ground turkey. Cook turkey until lightly browned and crumbly, and then add in oregano and frozen spinach. Reduce heat to low and heat the spinach a few minutes.

Remove from heat and begin assembling your tacos. Spread 1 tablespoon hummus across the bottom of each shell. Next, add turkey and spinach mixture. Top each taco with onion, cucumber, tomatoes, and olives. Garnish each taco with a little fresh feta.

ENCHILADA SUIZAS

Swiss cheese. In an enchilada. Love. I used to think enchiladas were too much hassle for a weeknight, but if you use my perfect chicken method they'll come together in no time!

INGREDIENTS

1 lb. cooked, shredded chicken
(see page 12 to see how I get it)
1 can cream of mushroom soup
1 4-oz. can chopped green chilies
salt and pepper
1 cup Swiss cheese, shredded (plus a little
extra for garnish)

$^1/_2$ cup Pepper Jack cheese, shredded
8 tortillas
1 15-oz. can tomatillo or green chili
enchilada sauce
chopped green onions to garnish

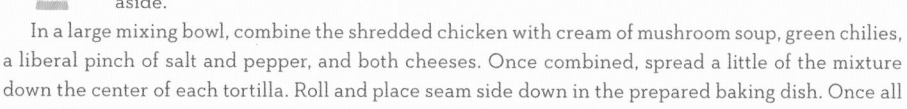

Preheat oven to 400° and lightly grease an 8 x 8-inch baking dish with cooking spray. Set aside.

In a large mixing bowl, combine the shredded chicken with cream of mushroom soup, green chilies, a liberal pinch of salt and pepper, and both cheeses. Once combined, spread a little of the mixture down the center of each tortilla. Roll and place seam side down in the prepared baking dish. Once all 8 enchiladas are tucked inside the dish, pour enchilada sauce over top.

Bake uncovered about 20 minutes, or until the edges are slightly browned and everything is bubbling. Remove from oven and garnish with chopped green onion and extra Swiss cheese.

BUFFALO CHICKEN PANINIS

FRI

I love grilling up chicken breasts for dinner one night and using the leftovers the next night in a completely different way. This summer, you should totally be grilling extra chicken each time you're out there. This sandwich makes for *the perfect quick weeknight meal*, post-swim supper, or dinner *when you just flat-out don't want to cook*. I use rye bread, but you can try sourdough, wheat, multigrain, French bread...whatever you have, it works.

INGREDIENTS

1 loaf of bakery bread, sliced
1 lb. grilled chicken, cut into bite-sized pieces
   or strips
½ cup of your favorite Buffalo hot sauce
2 cups spinach leaves
bleu cheese crumbles

Preheat your panini press or large skillet. Lightly grease with vegetable oil spray. In a bowl, toss grilled chicken with Buffalo sauce; set aside.

Take two slices of bread; top one slice with chicken, spinach, and a sprinkle of bleu cheese and then top with the second slice of bread. Place sandwich under the panini press for about 5 minutes or until golden and the cheese is melted. Slice in half and serve with your favorite chips.

If you don't have a panini press, just place each panini in a skillet over medium-high heat and set another skillet on top of your sandwich (to press it down). After about 4 minutes, flip your sandwich and press the other side down.

HAWAIIAN LUAU BUNDT CAKE

Even if you can't go to the islands, you can eat a cake that brings the island flavors to you. *Aloha.*

INGREDIENTS

1 box coconut cake mix
2 small boxes instant coconut pudding
   (use vanilla if you can't find it)
½ cup vegetable oil
1 15-oz. can crushed pineapple (reserve the
   juice!), divided
1 cup pineapple juice from your canned pineapple

¼ cup water (or more pineapple juice if
   your can has any left)
4 eggs
1 container cream cheese frosting
2 cups sweetened, flaked coconut, divided
Maraschino cherries to garnish (optional)

Preheat oven to 350° and grease a 10-inch Bundt pan. In mixing bowl, combine cake mix, puddings, oil, pineapple juice, water, and eggs with electric mixer. Stir in 1 cup crushed pineapple and one cup coconut. Pour into prepared pan and bake 40-45 minutes, or until toothpick inserted comes out clean. Let cake rest on counter in pan 10 minutes. Invert cake onto serving plate to finish cooling.

Stir remaining cup coconut into store-bought frosting and frost cooled cake. Top cake with cherries.

WEEK 2 SHOPPING LIST

PRODUCE

1 bulb garlic

4 cloves garlic

1 pint cherry tomatoes

2 cups spinach leaves

8-10 basil leaves

2 avocados

2 red onions

1 small onion

chopped green onions (garnish)

1 pkg. cabbage/slaw mix

1 lime

2-4 key limes

1 lemon

1 green bell pepper

1 jalapeno pepper

MEATS

10-12 slices bacon

1 lb. ground beef

1 lb. peeled and deveined shrimp

1 lb. ground turkey

1 lb. boneless, skinless chicken breasts (not frozen)

CANNED FOODS, CONDIMENTS, SOUPS, SAUCES

12 oz. chicken broth (1$\frac{1}{2}$ cups)

8 oz. chicken stock (1 cup)

1 1-oz. packet Ranch dressing seasoning mix

1 cup bottled Ranch dressing

CANNED FOODS, CONDIMENTS, SOUPS, SAUCES (CONT'D)

1 8-oz. jar sundried tomatoes in oil
2 4-oz. cans chopped green chilies
1 16- to 24-oz. jar salsa verde
guacamole (side or garnish)

FROZEN

1 pkg. frozen spinach

DAIRY

½ cup Parmesan cheese
feta cheese (garnish)
shredded Monterey Jack or Cheddar cheese (garnish)
4 eggs
1 8-oz. pkg. cream cheese

** Don't forget to stock up on your Pantry Essentials (see page 14)

GRAINS, PASTA, BREAD

1 lb. pasta (we use whole wheat penne)
burger buns (2 dinners)
8 tortillas
tortilla chips or strips

BAKING

1 box yellow cake mix
1 box (4 cups) powdered sugar

BLT PASTA

The roasted garlic is the star of this dish. Roasting your garlic makes the cloves tender and sweet while giving your dish a caramelized flavor that is delicious. The roasted garlic cloves will be extra tender and soft when you pull them from the bulb. A simple step gives a huge boost of flavor.

INGREDIENTS

1 bulb garlic
extra virgin olive oil
salt and pepper
1 pint cherry tomatoes
1 lb. pasta (we use whole wheat penne)
10-12 slices bacon, chopped

1 1/2 cups chicken broth
2 cups spinach leaves (just grab the kind next to the bagged salads)
1/2 cup Parmesan cheese, grated
8-10 basil leaves, torn or chopped

Preheat oven to 450°. Take your entire bulb of garlic and chop the top off, exposing the inside. Drizzle olive oil on top of exposed cloves and sprinkle liberal amounts of salt and pepper on top. Wrap entire bulb in foil and place on a baking sheet in the oven to roast for 30 minutes.

Take another baking sheet and spread out cherry tomatoes. Drizzle tomatoes with oil and sprinkle salt and pepper over all of them. After garlic has been in the oven 30 minutes, open oven door and move the garlic in foil onto the tomato baking sheet (so you only have one baking sheet in the oven now instead of two). Cook for an additional 15 minutes.

While the tomatoes and garlic are roasting, bring a large pot of water to boil. Cook pasta until al dente.

Meanwhile, set a skillet over medium-high heat and heat a couple tablespoons of olive oil. Once hot, add in chopped bacon to brown (about 6 minutes). At this point, unwrap the garlic from the foil and remove the roasted cloves with a fork. They will be really tender and smushy. Add in chicken stock and lots of salt and pepper to your bacon pan and deglaze the pan (scrape up the little bits from the bottom), lower the heat to medium-low, and simmer 3-5 minutes. Stir in spinach, roasted tomatoes, and roasted garlic pieces. Drain pasta and add to bacon mixture. Stir in cheese and basil.

RANCH BURGERS WITH AVOCADO RANCH SAUCE

Ranch burgers are pretty common, but add a little avocado ranch sauce and they're out of this world. *Easy. Simple. Weeknight. Done.*

INGREDIENTS

1 lb. ground beef
1 1-oz. packet Ranch dressing seasoning mix
1 avocado
1 cup bottled Ranch dressing
red onion slices
burger buns

Preheat your outdoor grill or indoor grill pan to medium-high. In a mixing bowl, combine ground beef with Ranch seasoning mix. Divide ground beef mixture into 4 burger patties. Grill about 6 minutes each side.

While the burgers are on the grill, place sliced avocado pieces in a food processor. Add in Ranch dressing and pulse until combined. (If you don't have a food processor, just use your hand mixer.) Remove burgers from the grill. Top bun with burger patty, avocado Ranch sauce, and sliced onion.

GRILLED SHRIMP TACOS

There is just something about summer and shrimp tacos. *They go together perfectly...* especially when enjoyed on a patio.

INGREDIENTS

1 lb. peeled and deveined shrimp
2 tablespoons chili powder
1 package cabbage/slaw mix (found by the prepackaged salads)
1 avocado, sliced
1 red onion, diced

1 lime, quartered
drizzle Ranch dressing
crushed tortilla chips or tortilla strips
tortillas

Preheat your outdoor grill or indoor grill pan to medium-high. In a bowl, combine shrimp and chili powder. Skewer your shrimp or put it in a fish/shrimp basket before placing it on your hot grill. Grill each side about a minute or two or until nice and charred.

Remove shrimp from grill and assemble tacos. We put down our tortillas first and then top it with a little slaw, some sliced avocado, a little red onion, a squirt of lime juice, a drizzle of Ranch, and a few pieces of tortilla chips for crunch.

SPINACH AND SUNDRIED TOMATO JOES

I took two of my favorite things—turkey meatballs and sloppy joes—and combined them into one. Such a simple, flavorful, and delicious supper.

INGREDIENTS

1 lb. ground turkey
4 cloves garlic, minced
1 package frozen spinach, thawed and drained of excess water
1 8-oz. jar sundried tomatoes in oil, drained
2 teaspoons lemon zest

feta cheese, crumbled to garnish
chopped green onions to garnish
salt and pepper
extra virgin olive oil
burger buns

In a large skillet over medium-high heat, brown your turkey in a drizzle of olive oil until browned and crumbly. Add in a liberal pinch of salt and pepper. Stir in your garlic, spinach, sundried tomatoes, and lemon zest. Reduce heat to medium and let simmer about 5 minutes or until everything is heated through.

Take each burger bun and top with a generous portion of ground turkey mixture. Garnish with feta cheese and chopped green onions.

CHICKEN CHILI VERDE

FRI

I love this meal because it cooks away all day in the slow cooker and then comes together in no time. *My kiddos love this* because they're into tortillas, chicken, salsa, and guacamole *(Texas kids for sure!)*.

INGREDIENTS

1 lb. boneless, skinless chicken breasts (not frozen)
1 green bell pepper, chopped
1 small onion, chopped
1 jalapeno pepper, seeded and chopped
2 4-oz. cans chopped green chilies
1 1-oz. package taco seasoning (about 2 tablespoons) or 2 tablespoons chili powder
1 16- to 24-oz. jar salsa verde

1 cup chicken stock or water
8 tortillas
guacamole as a side or to garnish
shredded Monterey Jack or Cheddar cheese to garnish
squeeze of fresh lime juice, optional

Combine chicken, bell pepper, onion, jalapeno pepper, cans of green chilies, taco seasoning, salsa, and stock or water in slow cooker. Cover and cook on low 6 to 8 hours or on high 3 to 4 hours.

When ready to serve, remove the lid of the slow cooker and shred up the chicken right inside the slow cooker using two forks. Top each tortilla with a little bit of the chicken mixture, some fresh guacamole, a little cheese, and a squeeze of lime juice.

KEY LIME PIE BARS

If you can't find *key limes* at your grocery store, use a regular lime instead. You'll need about 4 key limes or 2 regular limes for this recipe.

INGREDIENTS

1 box yellow cake mix
4 eggs
½ cup butter, melted
1 box powdered sugar (about 4 cups)

1 8-oz. package cream cheese, softened
2 tablespoons key lime zest
4 tablespoons fresh key lime juice

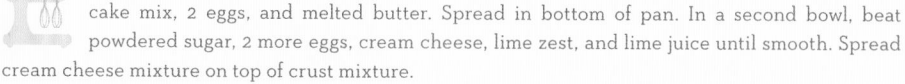

Preheat oven to 350° and grease a 9 x 13-inch baking dish. In a large mixing bowl, combine cake mix, 2 eggs, and melted butter. Spread in bottom of pan. In a second bowl, beat powdered sugar, 2 more eggs, cream cheese, lime zest, and lime juice until smooth. Spread cream cheese mixture on top of crust mixture.

Bake 35-40 minutes until edges are brown and center is set (it will still be slightly wobbly in the middle). Cool on counter 30 minutes, then refrigerate 2 hours or up to 2 days.

FAMILY FAVORITES

MIX AND MATCH IDEAS

. . . .

. . . .

. . . .

. . . .

. . . .

. . . .

FALL

WEEK ONE MENU

MONDAY	BBQ Apple Chicken Sandwiches
TUESDAY	Sweet Potato Shepherd's Pie
WEDNESDAY	Mexican Minestrone
THURSDAY	Crunchy BBQ Brisket Tacos
FRIDAY	Sausage and Broccoli Tortellini Bake
SOMETHING SWEET	Pumpkin Spice Cupcakes

WEEK TWO MENU

MONDAY	Enchilada Chili
TUESDAY	Chicken à la King
WEDNESDAY	Brown Sugar Brisket
THURSDAY	Sausage and Butternut Squash Pasta
FRIDAY	Pizza Meatballs
SOMETHING SWEET	Caramel Apple Bread Pudding

WEEK 1 SHOPPING LIST

PRODUCE

3 onions (1 optional)
2 cups mashed sweet potatoes
3 cloves garlic
10 to 12 green onions
2 cups broccolini

MEATS

2 lb. boneless, skinless chicken breasts
1 lb. ground beef
1 2-3 lb. brisket
1 lb. Italian sausage

CANNED FOODS, CONDIMENTS, SOUPS, SAUCES

2 cups apple juice or cider
1 16-oz. bottle BBQ sauce
1 10-oz. can cream of mushroom soup
1 15-oz. can black beans
1 15-oz. can Great Northern beans
24 oz. chicken stock
1 10-oz. can Rotel tomatoes
2 cups salsa
1 to 2 cups BBQ sauce

GRAINS, PASTA, BREAD

toast, burger buns, or rolls

2 cups of a short-cut pasta (we use a mix of penne and shells for fun)

crunchy taco shells

2 9-oz. pkgs. cheese-filled tortellini or ravioli

BAKING

1 cup breadcrumbs

1 tablespoon cinnamon or pumpkin pie spice

1 15-oz. can pumpkin purée

1 cup pumpkin spice chips (optional)

4 cups powdered sugar

FROZEN

1½ cups frozen corn

1 10-oz. pkg. frozen peas and carrots

DAIRY

3 tablespoons milk, half and half, or cream

½ cup Parmesan cheese

4 eggs

1 8-oz. pkg. cream cheese

Monterey Jack cheese (garnish)

Cheddar cheese to (garnish)

** Don't forget to stock up on your Pantry Essentials (see page 14)

BBQ APPLE CHICKEN SANDWICHES

I just adore a slow-cooker meal that is super simple and waiting when I'm ready to eat. Apples, onions, and slow cookers are staples at our house in the fall! The *apple juice adds sweetness* to this dish without being overpowering, and the *chicken cooks up juicy and tender.*

INGREDIENTS

1 lb. boneless, skinless chicken breasts,
   frozen or thawed
2 cups apple juice or cider
1 16-oz bottle BBQ sauce
1 onion, sliced and sautéed (optional)
toast, burger buns, or rolls to serve

In your slow cooker, combine chicken, apple juice or cider, and entire bottle of BBQ sauce. Cook on low 6-8 hours or on high 3-4 hours. When dinner is ready, remove chicken and some sauce from slow cooker into a bowl. Shred chicken with two forks (add in a little more sauce if needed). Serve shredded chicken with sautéed onions (optional) on top of your favorite bread.

SWEET POTATO SHEPHERD'S PIE

Have no fear if sweet potatoes aren't your thing: You can totally substitute a basic mashed potato instead! This is a super simple weeknight meal—*meat and potatoes all in one place.*

INGREDIENTS

1 lb. ground beef
1 onion, chopped
1 10-oz. can cream of mushroom soup
1 10-oz. pkg. frozen peas and carrots

2 cups mashed sweet potatoes
extra virgin olive oil
salt and pepper

Preheat oven to 400°. In a large skillet over medium-high heat, brown ground beef in a drizzle of olive oil until crumbly; drain fat. Stir in onion and sauté a few minutes. Add in a generous pinch of salt and pepper. Reduce heat to low and stir in cream of mushroom soup and frozen veggies. When combined, pour mixture into a greased 8 x 8-inch baking dish. Spread mashed potatoes all over the top, covering the meat completely.

Pop casserole into the oven and bake about 15 minutes, or until everything is bubbly. Remove from oven and serve.

MEXICAN MINESTRONE

I'm always thinking of ways to make different versions of soups at our house. In the fall and winter, you'll find us eating soup at least twice a week for supper. *This is a south-of-the-border take* on a traditional Italian soup.

INGREDIENTS

- 1 lb. chicken breasts, frozen or thawed
- 1 15-oz. can black beans, drained and rinsed
- 1 15-oz. can Great Northern Beans, drained and rinsed
- 2 cups chicken stock
- 1 10-oz. can Rotel tomatoes, undrained
- 1 onion, chopped

- 2 tablespoons chili powder or 1 packet of taco seasoning
- 1½ cups frozen corn
- 2 cups short-cut pasta (I used a mix of penne and shells for fun), uncooked
- chopped green onion and/or Cheddar cheese to garnish

In your slow cooker, combine chicken, rinsed and drained beans, chicken stock, Rotel tomatoes, onion, and chili powder. Cover and cook on high 3 to 4 hours or on low 6 to 8 hours. About 30 minutes before serving, remove lid and shred chicken right inside the slow cooker using two forks. Stir in frozen corn and pasta. Replace lid, turn the slow cooker to high, and cook another 30 minutes or so.

Ladle soup into bowls and garnish with chopped green onion and/or Cheddar cheese.

CRUNCHY BBQ BRISKET TACOS

You'll come home from a busy day and *your brisket will be all cooked up and tender in the slow cooker.* All you do is add a little BBQ sauce and a few garnishes and you're done!

INGREDIENTS

extra virgin olive oil
salt and pepper
1 2- to 3-lb. brisket
2 cups salsa
1-1½ cups water

1-2 cups BBQ sauce
crunchy taco shells
chopped green onions and/or Monterey
  Jack cheese to garnish

Preheat.a heavy pot with olive oil over medium-high heat. Salt and pepper the brisket, and brown each side in the pot 4-5 minutes. Make sure you salt and pepper each side. Transfer brisket to a slow cooker and pour salsa over the top. Pour a little water over everything until the brisket is mostly covered in the salsa and water. Cover and cook on low 7-8 hours or on high 4-5 hours.

About 20 minutes before serving, remove brisket to cutting board and cover with foil. This will allow the meat to rest and the juices to redistribute and keep it moist. Discard all of the liquid in the slow cooker.

After your brisket has cooled about 10 minutes, slice and chop it into pieces and place those pieces into a bowl. Once all of your chopped beef is in a bowl, add BBQ sauce and coat everything. Use as much BBQ sauce as you think your family will love.

Take each taco shell (you should get 6 to 8, depending on how much brisket you use) and stuff it with your brisket mixture. Finally, garnish your tacos with some shredded cheese and chopped onions.

SAUSAGE AND BROCCOLI TORTELLINI BAKE

This casserole is fast and simple. I chopped up some broccolini for this version, but you can use broccoli florets, cauliflower, or asparagus. This method is all about assembly: Grab some broccolini, grab some sausage (or even a brat!), grab some refrigerated tortellini (ravioli works too), *assemble, bake, and eat.*

INGREDIENTS

2 9-oz. packages cheese-filled tortellini or ravioli
1 lb. Italian sausage
extra virgin olive oil
3 cloves garlic, chopped
8-10 green onions, chopped

1 cup chicken stock
2 cups chopped broccolini
2 tablespoons milk, half and half, or cream
1 cup breadcrumbs
½ cup Parmesan cheese, grated

Preheat oven to 400° and grease an 8 x 8-inch inch baking dish. Bring a large pot of water to a boil. Drop in tortellini and cook about 5 minutes. Drain water and set tortellini aside.

Meanwhile, in a large skillet over medium-high heat, cook up sausage in a drizzle of olive oil. Once sausage is brown and crumbly, add garlic, green onions, and chicken stock. Reduce heat to low and let your mixture simmer just a minute or two. Add broccolini and reserved tortellini. Stir in milk. Pour sausage mixture into prepared baking dish. Sprinkle breadcrumbs and Parmesan cheese over the top. Bake about 15 minutes uncovered or until the casserole is bubbling and a little brown around the edges. Remove from oven and serve.

To make in advance, assemble the casserole but don't bake it. At this point, you could cover and refrigerate the casserole or freeze it. You will need to adjust your baking time to about 25 minutes if it's coming from the fridge or 40 minutes if it's coming from the freezer.

PUMPKIN SPICE CUPCAKES

A little pumpkin, a little spice, *a lot of yummy!*

INGREDIENTS

2 cups sugar
1½ cups vegetable oil
4 eggs
2 cups flour
1 teaspoon salt
2 teaspoons baking soda
1 tablespoon cinnamon or pumpkin pie spice

1 15-oz. can pumpkin purée
1 cup pumpkin spice chips, optional
1 8-oz. package cream cheese, softened
½ cup butter, softened
1 teaspoon vanilla
4 cups powdered sugar
1 tablespoon milk

Preheat oven to 350°. Line 3 (12-count) muffin tins with cupcake liners or spray one 9 x 13-inch baking dish with cooking spray; set aside.

In a mixing bowl combine sugar, vegetable oil, and eggs with an electric mixer; set aside. In a separate mixing bowl, combine flour, salt, baking soda, and cinnamon with a fork or whisk. Slowly beat the flour mixture into the sugar mixture. Mix until just combined. Next, beat in pumpkin until just combined. Stir in your pumpkin chips (optional).

Pour batter into prepared baking dish or divide between your muffin tins. Bake cupcakes 14-16 minutes, or until a toothpick inserted in the middle comes out clean. If you're using a 9 x 13-inch baking dish, bake about 40 minutes. Allow to cool completely before frosting.

To make the frosting, beat the cream cheese, butter, vanilla, powdered sugar, and milk together. Add more milk if the frosting is too thick and more powdered sugar if it's too thin. Frost cooled cupcakes and store in fridge if not serving immediately.

WEEK 2 SHOPPING LIST

PRODUCE

$4^1/_2$ onions
6 cloves garlic
handful chopped basil (optional)
2 Granny Smith apples
green onion (garnish)

CANNED FOODS, CONDIMENTS, SOUPS, SAUCES

1 14-oz. can Rotel tomatoes
1 10-oz. can enchilada sauce
1 15-oz. can mild chili beans
1 can cream of chicken soup
4 oz. chicken stock ($1/_2$ cup)
1 14-oz. jar pizza sauce
4 cups apple juice

MEATS

1 lb. ground beef, turkey, or chicken
1 lb. sausage (pork or chicken)
$1^1/_2$ lbs. boneless, skinless
chicken breasts
1 3- to 5-lb. flat-trimmed brisket
1 lb. ground beef
$1/_2$ cup pepperoni

GRAINS, PASTA, BREAD

biscuits or toast

1 lb. pasta

1 loaf challah or brioche

tortilla chips (garnish)

FROZEN

$2\frac{1}{2}$ cups frozen corn

1 cup frozen peas

1 12-oz. box frozen butternut squash

BAKING

$1\frac{1}{2}$ cup brown sugar

1 tablespoon cinnamon

1 cup pecan pieces

1 12-oz. jar caramel topping

1 tablespoon fennel seed (optional)

DAIRY

2 tablespoons milk

1 cup Cheddar cheese

Cheddar cheese (garnish)

$\frac{1}{2}$ cup Mozzarella cheese

2 eggs

Parmesan cheese (garnish)

4 cups milk

3 eggs

sour cream (garnish)

** Don't forget to stock up on your Pantry Essentials
(see page 14)

ENCHILADA CHILI

MON

This chili is great because it's a One-Pound Meal (meaning you can use ground beef, ground turkey or ground chicken), *it's a One-Pot Meal* (you won't have other dirty dishes to clean up), it comes together in minutes, and it's really delicious!

INGREDIENTS

1 lb. ground beef, turkey, or chicken
extra virgin olive oil
salt and pepper
1 tablespoon chili powder
1 onion, chopped
1 14-oz can Rotel tomatoes

1 10-oz can enchilada sauce
1½ cups frozen corn
1 15-oz. can mild chili beans, undrained
tortilla chips, shredded cheese, chopped green
   onion, sour cream to garnish

In a large pot over medium-high heat, brown ground meat in a drizzle of olive oil with a pinch of salt and pepper. Once brown, stir in chili powder and chopped onion and sauté a few minutes. Stir in Rotel, enchilada sauce, corn, and beans. Reduce heat to low and cook about 10 minutes. Ladle chili into bowls and garnish with your favorite toppings.

CHICKEN À LA KING

You can be totally versatile on your carb choices. I like a traditional biscuit with mine, but you can use toast, cornbread, or an English muffin—or be like my hubby and go without! *This meal is simple and happy—perfect for family suppers.*

INGREDIENTS

1½ lb. boneless, skinless chicken breasts, frozen or thawed
½ onion, chopped
1 can cream of chicken soup
2 tablespoons flour

1 cup frozen peas
1 cup frozen corn
salt and pepper
biscuits or toast for serving

Layer the first 4 ingredients in your slow cooker. Give it a quick stir and then cover and cook on low 6-7 hours or on high 3-4 hours.

About 30 minutes before serving, take two forks and shred the chicken right inside your slow cooker. Next, stir in frozen peas and corn with a generous pinch of salt and pepper. Cover and cook on high another 20-30 minutes. Spoon chicken mixture over the top of your biscuits and serve.

BROWN SUGAR BRISKET

WED

This brisket is particularly yummy because it has a *brown sugar and mustard glaze* over it. I serve this with baked potatoes and a green salad, but mashed potatoes would be yummy too! Or pile this up on a bun and serve it as a sandwich with a side of potato salad or chips. As for the leftovers, add some brisket and Monterey Jack cheese to a tortilla and make a quesadilla or taco. I used apple juice as my cooking liquid because it adds great flavor to the meat, but you can cut the amount of apple juice in half by using water too.

INGREDIENTS

1 3- to 5-lb. flat-trimmed brisket
1/2 cup brown sugar
1 tablespoon yellow mustard
1 onion, chopped

4 cups apple juice (or 2 cups apple juice
   and 2 cups water)
salt and pepper
extra virgin olive oil

Season brisket with salt and pepper. Heat olive oil in a large skillet over medium-high heat and brown each side of your brisket, about 4 minutes per side. While it's browning, combine the brown sugar and mustard together in a small bowl; set aside.

Place browned brisket in the slow cooker. Rub brown sugar mixture all over the brisket. Add in chopped onion and pour apple juice on top. Cover and cook on high about 8 hours.

When you're ready to eat, open the lid and remove the brisket from the liquid (discard the liquid) to a cutting board. Shred the brisket and serve.

SAUSAGE AND BUTTERNUT SQUASH PASTA

Check your freezer department for a box of frozen butternut squash. All you do is bring it home and defrost it. If you would rather *roast your own squash*, see below for directions.

INGREDIENTS

1 lb. sausage (pork or chicken)
1 lb. pasta
1 onion, chopped
3 cloves garlic, chopped
1 tablespoon fennel seed (optional)
½ cup chicken stock

2 tablespoons flour
2 tablespoons milk
1 12-oz. box frozen butternut squash, defrosted
1 cup Cheddar cheese, grated
handful chopped basil, optional

Over medium-high heat, brown sausage until cooked through and crumbly; drain fat. Add in onions and garlic and sauté about 5 minutes. Meanwhile, bring a large pot of water to a boil, drop in pasta, and cook to al dente (about 7-8 minutes).

Stir the fennel seed into sausage and add chicken stock to deglaze your pan (scrape all the little bits off the bottom). Simmer over low heat a minute or two.

Whisk flour and milk into sausage for a minute to create a roux. Stir in defrosted squash and cheese. Reduce heat to low and let everything simmer together about 5 minutes.

Drain pasta and add to sausage mixture. Stir until all the pasta is covered in sauce. Top with basil (optional).

Note: Roasting your own butternut squash is simple! Preheat your oven to 425°. Split a butternut squash down the middle, scrape out the seeds, drizzle a few tablespoons of extra virgin olive oil over the tops, and season liberally with salt and pepper. Roast on a baking sheet in the oven about 30 minutes. Remove from oven and scrape out the insides of your squash. Stir about 2 cups of that squash into this pasta dinner.

PIZZA MEATBALLS

My kids love pizza and they love meatballs, so I made some *meatballs that taste like pizza!* My hubby and I eat our meatballs with a side salad but my kiddos have theirs over buttered noodles. No matter how you serve them, they'll eat them.

INGREDIENTS

1 lb. ground beef
1 onion, chopped
2-3 cloves of garlic, chopped
2 tablespoons Italian seasoning
½ cup Mozzarella cheese, shredded

2 eggs
½ cup pepperoni, chopped
1 14-oz. jar pizza sauce
Parmesan cheese, grated to garnish

Preheat oven to 425°. Line a baking sheet with foil and spray with cooking spray; set aside. In a large mixing bowl, combine ground beef, onion, garlic, Italian seasoning, cheese, eggs, and pepperoni. Shape the meat mixture into 12 golf-ball-sized meatballs. Place meatballs on prepared pan and roast 15 to 18 minutes or until lightly browned. Remove from oven and drizzle pizza sauce on top with a sprinkle of Parmesan.

CARAMEL APPLE BREAD PUDDING

If you've never made bread pudding before, this is your chance. It's *warm and cozy and perfect for chilly nights*. I made this bread pudding for dinner guests and then served it in mason jars instead of bowls or plates. Served alone, with a dollop of whipped cream, or a scoop of ice cream—you can't go wrong!

INGREDIENTS

1 loaf challah or brioche, torn into pieces
4 cups milk
3 eggs, lightly beaten
1 cup grated apples (I used 2 Granny Smiths and grated them with my cheese grater, or substitute 1 cup applesauce)

1 cup sugar
1 cup brown sugar
1 tablespoon cinnamon
1 cup pecan pieces
1 12-oz. jar caramel topping, divided

Preheat oven to 350° and grease a 9 x 13-inch baking dish. Tear bread into bite-sized pieces and place them in baking dish. Pour milk over bread and let stand about 10 minutes.

Stir eggs together with the grated apple, sugar, brown sugar, cinnamon, pecan pieces, and $^1/_2$ cup caramel topping. Pour this mixture over bread mixture. Bake uncovered for 40 to 45 minutes.

Remove from oven and serve immediately. I cut mine into portions and then drizzle additional caramel topping over each piece. If you're serving this in a mason jar or trifle dish, drizzle caramel in between layers of bread pudding.

FAMILY FAVORITES

MIX AND MATCH IDEAS

WINTER

WEEK ONE MENU

MONDAY	Beef Enchiladas
TUESDAY	Spaghetti and Meat Sauce
WEDNESDAY	Italian Brisket Sandwiches
THURSDAY	Spinach and Chicken Noodle Soup
FRIDAY	Beer Chicken Chili
SOMETHING SWEET	Cherry Berry Cobbler

WEEK TWO MENU

MONDAY	Mom's Meatloaf
TUESDAY	Creamy Tomato Chicken Pasta
WEDNESDAY	Beefy Cornbread Casserole
THURSDAY	Pepperoni Pizza Soup
FRIDAY	Chicken Citrus Tostadas
SOMETHING SWEET	Butterfinger Blondies

WEEK 1 SHOPPING LIST

PRODUCE

4 onions

green onions (garnish)

1 pint cherry tomatoes

6 cloves garlic

basil (garnish x2)

1 red bell pepper

1 jalapeno pepper

MEATS

1 lb. ground beef

1 lb. ground beef or turkey

1 3- to 5-lb. brisket

2 lbs. boneless, skinless chicken breasts

8 slices bacon

CANNED FOODS, CONDIMENTS, SOUPS, SAUCES

1 4-oz. can chopped black olives

1 10-oz. can cream of mushroom soup

1 10-oz. can enchilada sauce

2 28-oz. cans whole peeled tomatoes

1 cup beef or chicken stock

1 8-oz. can tomato sauce

40 oz. chicken stock

2 10-oz. cans cream of chicken soup

1 16-oz. can chili beans

1 cup beer

GRAINS, PASTA, BREAD

6-8 tortillas (flour or whole wheat)
1 lb. spaghetti noodles
burger buns
2 cups short-cut pasta

FROZEN

1 10-oz. pkg. frozen spinach
1 10-oz. pkg. frozen mixed berries

BAKING

1 tablespoon brown sugar
1 21-oz. can cherry pie filling
1 yellow cake mix

DAIRY

2 cups Cheddar cheese
Parmesan cheese (garnish x2)
Cheddar cheese (garnish x2)
ice cream (optional)

** Don't forget to stock up on your Pantry Essentials
(see page 14)

BEEF ENCHILADAS

These enchiladas are delicious—and they are so simple too! *These are a huge hit at our house,* and it's a great dish for a potluck supper or freezer meal.

INGREDIENTS

- 1 lb. ground beef
- 1 onion, chopped
- 1 4-oz. can chopped black olives, drained (optional)
- 2 cups Cheddar cheese, shredded
- 6-8 tortillas (flour or whole wheat)
- 1 10-oz. can cream of mushroom soup
- 1 10-oz. can enchilada sauce

Preheat oven to 350°. Lightly spray an 8 x 8-inch baking dish with cooking spray; set aside. In a large skillet over medium-high heat, cook ground beef until brown and crumbly; drain fat. Stir in chopped onion and sauté another 4-5 minutes. Add olives and ¾ of your cheese and stir until everything is melted together. Take each tortilla and spoon some of the cheesy ground beef mixture down the center. Roll up and place seam side down in prepared baking dish.

In a small bowl, combine mushroom soup and enchilada sauce together with a spoon. Pour this mixture over enchiladas in the pan. Sprinkle remaining cheese over the enchiladas. Bake 30-40 minutes or until bubbly. Remove from oven and serve.

SPAGHETTI AND MEAT SAUCE

TUE

Does any meal say *family supper* more than spaghetti and meat sauce? You can use either ground beef or ground turkey in this recipe. *Simple and satisfying!*

INGREDIENTS

1 pint cherry tomatoes
extra virgin olive oil
salt and pepper
1 lb. spaghetti noodles
1 lb. ground beef or turkey

1 onion, chopped
3 cloves garlic, chopped
1 28-oz. can whole peeled tomatoes
1 tablespoon Italian seasoning
Parmesan cheese and basil to garnish, optional

Preheat oven to 425°. On a foil-lined baking sheet, spread cherry tomatoes out. Drizzle olive oil over the tomatoes and sprinkle liberally with salt and pepper. Roast in the oven about 15 minutes. (You can omit this step if you like and just add an extra can of tomatoes into your meat sauce, but I love the added flavor of the roasted tomatoes.)

Over medium-high heat, bring a large pot of water to a boil; add noodles and cook until al dente (about 8 minutes).

Meanwhile, over medium-high heat, brown your ground beef or turkey in a skillet with a drizzle of olive oil and some salt and pepper. Once browned and crumbly, drain fat and then add onions and garlic and sauté a couple of minutes. Turn heat to low and add the can of whole peeled tomatoes and Italian seasoning. With wooden spoon, gently break up the whole tomatoes in your skillet. At this time, add the roasted cherry tomatoes and gently break them up too.

I like to stir a little basil and Parmesan right into my meat sauce, but you could wait and use them as garnish instead. Drain the pasta and add to meat sauce. Serve with a sprinkle of Parmesan and a little basil.

ITALIAN BRISKET SANDWICHES

Brisket is such an easy cut of meat to cook in the slow cooker, so we eat it often...especially during the fall and winter. These open-faced sandwiches are *super simple and really yummy!*

INGREDIENTS

1 3- to 5-pound brisket
extra virgin olive oil
salt and pepper
2 tablespoons Italian seasoning
1 onion, chopped
3 cloves garlic (leave whole)
1 28-oz. can whole peeled tomatoes

1 cup beef stock, chicken stock, or water
1 8-oz. can tomato sauce
1 tablespoon brown sugar
1 tablespoon Worcestershire sauce
burger buns
grated Parmesan cheese to garnish
basil to garnish

In a large pan over medium-high heat, brown both sides of your brisket in a tablespoon of oil, about 3 minutes per side. Sprinkle salt and pepper liberally over each side.

Once browned, put brisket in slow cooker. Sprinkle Italian seasoning over the brisket and add onion, whole garlic cloves, can of whole tomatoes, and stock (or water). Cover and cook on high about 8 hours.

An hour before you're ready to eat, combine tomato sauce, brown sugar, and Worcestershire sauce in a small bowl. Set aside. Remove brisket from the slow cooker to a cutting board; drain everything out of the slow cooker. Return the brisket to the hot slow cooker and shred it up using two forks. Pour tomato sauce mixture over everything, cover, and continue cooking another 30 minutes-1 hour.

When you're ready to serve, top each bun with some of the shredded brisket, a sprinkle of Parmesan, and some basil.

SPINACH AND CHICKEN NOODLE SOUP

I'm such a sucker for a good bowl of soup. I make this one in the slow cooker so my house smells yummy all day. *Warm. Hearty. Comforting. Soup.*

INGREDIENTS

3 cups chicken stock
1 onion, chopped
2 10-oz. cans cream of chicken soup
1 10-oz. package of frozen spinach, thawed and all excess water squeezed out

salt and pepper
1 lb. boneless, skinless chicken breasts (uncooked)
2 cups uncooked short-cut pasta (shells, rigatoni, and penne all work)
shredded Cheddar cheese to garnish

In your slow cooker, layer the first 6 ingredients. Cover and cook on low 6 or 7 hours or on high about 3 hours.

About 30 minutes before you're ready to eat, remove the lid, shred the chicken right inside the slow cooker using two forks, and pour pasta in. Cover and continue to cook about 30 minutes or until the noodles are tender. *Try not to remove the lid during that 30 minutes or it will take your noodles a lot longer to cook.*

When the noodles are cooked, ladle into bowls and garnish with a little cheese.

BEER CHICKEN CHILI

This stove-top chili is the perfect ending to a cozy week. *Full of flavor but not a lot of work!*

INGREDIENTS

1 lb. chicken breasts
extra virgin olive oil
salt and pepper
8 slices bacon, chopped
1 red bell pepper, chopped
1 jalapeno pepper, seeded and chopped

2 tablespoons chili powder
1 16-oz. can chili beans, undrained
1 cup beer
2 cups chicken stock
chopped green onions to garnish
shredded Cheddar cheese to garnish

Chop chicken into bite-sized pieces. Set aside. In a large pot over medium-high heat, drizzle in a tablespoon or so of olive oil. Add in chopped chicken and a big pinch of salt and pepper. Allow chicken to brown on both sides, about 5 minutes. Once brown, add bacon and allow to crisp.

Next, add bell pepper and jalapeno pepper and sauté 1-2 minutes. Add in chili powder and chili beans. Stir in beer and stock, reduce heat to medium-low, and simmer about 10 minutes, stirring occasionally.

When ready to serve, ladle into bowls and garnish with green onions and shredded cheese. That's it! The beer adds a nice depth of flavor, but the alcohol burns off and makes this a family meal.

CHERRY BERRY COBBLER

I just cannot stop making this cobbler. It's simple to make and delicious every time. After a special meal, *enjoy this delicious cobbler with the ones you love.*

INGREDIENTS

1 10-oz. package frozen mixed berries
   (do not thaw)
1 21-oz. can cherry pie filling
1 yellow cake mix
$^1/_2$ cup butter, melted
ice cream, optional

Preheat oven to 350° and grease a 9 x 13-inch baking dish. Spread frozen berries across bottom of dish. Next, spoon pie filling on top of the frozen berries and then sprinkle the box of dry cake mix over the pie filling. Finally, drizzle the melted butter over everything.

Bake uncovered 55-60 minutes. Remove from oven and serve immediately (with a little ice cream if you desire). I promise...you'll make it once and then make it over and over again.

WEEK 2 SHOPPING LIST

PRODUCE
4 onions
8 green onions
basil (garnish x2)
1 green bell pepper
3 oranges

MEATS
2 lbs. ground beef
1 lb. ground beef, chicken, or turkey
2 lbs. boneless chicken breasts
2 cups pepperoni

CANNED FOODS, CONDIMENTS, SOUPS, SAUCES
1 8-oz. can tomato sauce
8 oz. chicken stock
1 10-oz. can tomato soup
1 28-oz. can crushed tomatoes
1 14-oz. can diced tomatoes
1 6-oz. can tomato paste
1 1-oz. packet powdered Italian dressing mix
1 cup BBQ sauce
ground fennel (optional)

GRAINS, PASTA, BREAD

$^1\!/_2$ lb. of pasta

1 can refrigerated biscuits

4-6 tostada shells

1 cup Saltine cracker crumbs
(about 12 crackers)

BAKING

1 cup brown sugar

1 8-oz. pkg. cornbread mix (I use Jiffy)

1 box yellow cake mix

5 regular-sized Butterfingers

3 cups powdered sugar

DAIRY

6 eggs

4 oz. cream cheese (half a block)

1 cup milk

$1^1\!/_2$ cups Mozzarella cheese

1 cup Parmesan cheese

Parmesan cheese (garnish)

Cheddar cheese (garnish)

Sour cream (garnish)

** Don't forget to stock up on your Pantry Essentials
(see page 14)

MOM'S MEATLOAF

This is my husband's favorite meal. Period. Favorite. It can be prepared in advance and popped in the oven at the last minute, and *you probably already have all of the ingredients on hand.* Served with a side of mashed potatoes, this is a man's dinner. A real man's dinner.

INGREDIENTS

1 lb. ground beef
1 cup Saltine cracker crumbs (about 12 crackers)
2 eggs, beaten
1 onion, chopped
1 teaspoon salt

5 tablespoons Worcestershire sauce, divided
1 8-oz. can tomato sauce
1 cup ketchup
2/3 cup brown sugar
1 teaspoon mustard

Preheat oven to 350°. Mix ground beef, cracker crumbs, eggs, onion, salt, 3 tablespoons Worcestershire sauce, and tomato sauce in a bowl. Put in a greased 8 x 8-inch baking dish and bake 40 minutes.

Meanwhile, combine remaining 2 tablespoons Worcestershire sauce, ketchup, brown sugar, and mustard in a bowl. Once 40 minutes is up, top casserole with sauce and return to oven for an additional 15 minutes.

CREAMY TOMATO CHICKEN PASTA

I think *the key to a good slow cooker meal is adding a little freshness at the end.* The grated cheese and fresh basil really brighten up this supper. Sometimes, I'll cook the pasta in the slow cooker but in this recipe you really don't want the pasta to absorb all of the sauce, so I cook up the pasta right before serving.

INGREDIENTS

1 lb. uncooked chicken breasts (frozen or defrosted)
1 cup chicken stock (or water)
1 1-oz. packet powdered Italian dressing mix
1 onion, chopped
1 10-oz. can tomato soup

1 14-oz. can diced tomatoes
4 oz. cream cheese (half a block)
1/2 lb. pasta, cooked
grated Parmesan cheese to garnish
fresh basil to garnish

In your slow cooker, combine chicken, stock, packet of dry seasoning mix, onion, tomato soup, and diced tomatoes. Cover and cook on low 6-8 hours or on high about 3 hours.

Half an hour before serving, remove lid and shred the chicken right inside the slow cooker using two forks. Turn the heat to high and add cream cheese. Replace the lid and cook on high the last 30 minutes.

Right before you serve, add your hot, cooked pasta to the slow cooker and stir everything together. Ladle pasta into bowls and garnish with some grated Parmesan and fresh basil.

BEEFY CORNBREAD CASSEROLE

This is just one *of those feel-good suppers*. It's a simple and hearty dinner for your family!

INGREDIENTS

1 lb. ground beef, chicken, or turkey
1 onion, chopped
1½ cups ketchup
¼ cup brown sugar
2 tablespoons Worcestershire sauce
1 tablespoon chili powder

1 8-oz. package cornbread mix (I use Jiffy)
½ cup milk
1 egg
sour cream and/or shredded Cheddar cheese to garnish

Preheat oven to 350°. Grease an 8 x 8-inch baking dish and set aside. In a large skillet over medium-high heat, brown ground beef and onion until cooked and crumbly; drain fat. Stir in the next 4 ingredients and reduce heat to low. Simmer together about 5 minutes and then pour beef mixture into prepared baking dish.

In a small bowl, mix dry cornbread mix with milk and egg. Pour batter over ground beef mixture. Bake uncovered about 20 minutes or until cornbread is browned on the edges and the casserole is bubbly. Remove from oven and let stand 5 minutes before cutting into squares and garnishing with sour cream and/or shredded cheese.

This recipe serves 4 adults but could be easily doubled and prepared in a 9 x 13-inch baking dish.

THU

PEPPERONI PIZZA SOUP

Make this soup the way you like it! You can *make it in the slow cooker or on the stove*, you can use any ground meat you like, and if you like other meats or veggies on your pizza, add them!

INGREDIENTS

1 lb. ground beef
2 tablespoons Italian seasoning
pinch ground fennel (optional)
1 onion, chopped
1 green bell pepper, chopped
1 6-oz. can tomato paste

1 28-oz. can crushed tomatoes
2 cups sliced pepperoni
1½ cups Mozzarella cheese, shredded
    basil to garnish
1 can refrigerated biscuits
1 cup Parmesan cheese, grated

Slow cooker directions: In a skillet, brown ground beef; drain fat. Place the meat in a slow cooker and then add the next six ingredients. Cook on low 6-8 hours or on high 3-4 hours. When ready to serve, stir in pepperoni and garnish with mozzarella and basil. Serve with biscuit (see below).

Stovetop directions: In a large pot, cook ground beef over medium-high heat until brown and crumbly; drain fat. Stir in seasonings, onion, and bell pepper. Sauté a few minutes. Stir in tomato paste and crushed tomatoes. Reduce heat to low and simmer about 10 minutes. Break up the crushed tomatoes with a wooden spoon as you occasionally stir. Add in the pepperoni slices. Ladle soup into bowls and serve with Mozzarella cheese and basil. Top with a biscuit.

To make biscuits, follow the directions on the can of biscuits. Before you place the biscuits in the oven, brush the tops with a little butter or olive oil and sprinkle Parmesan cheese on top. Bake according to package directions and serve.

CHICKEN CITRUS TOSTADAS

FRI

Citrus fruits are in season, so it's the perfect time to marry them with other flavors for dinner. You could also use corn, flour, or crunchy taco shells instead of a tostada.

INGREDIENTS

1 lb. cooked, shredded chicken (see page 12)
1 cup fresh orange juice (about 2 juicy oranges)
1 cup of your favorite BBQ sauce

8 green onions, chopped
4-6 tostada shells
orange slices to garnish

In a small bowl, combine orange juice and BBQ sauce until combined. Pour this sauce over cooked and shredded chicken. Scoop out a generous portion of chicken onto each tostada shell and sprinkle a few green onions on top. Garnish with an orange wedge or two. If you're feeling extra fancy, add a little shredded Pepper Jack cheese on top.

BUTTERFINGER BLONDIES

These are just fabulous. I *mixed and matched my favorite bar recipe* and added chopped Butterfingers. Not only are these really simple, they're really yummy too!

INGREDIENTS

1 box yellow cake mix
½ cup vegetable oil
3 eggs
5 regular-sized Butterfingers, chopped
(about 3 cups)

½ cup butter, softened
3 cups powdered sugar
splash of milk

Preheat oven to 350° and grease a 9 x 13-inch baking dish; set aside. In a mixing bowl, combine cake mix, vegetable oil, and eggs with an electric mixer. Stir in one cup chopped Butterfingers. Pour batter into prepared pan and bake 20 minutes or until a toothpick inserted in the middle comes out clean.

While the bars are cooling, prepare frosting. In a mixing bowl, combine butter and powdered sugar with milk. Add more powdered sugar if it's too thin or more milk if it's too thick. Once your frosting reaches the desired consistency, stir in remaining 2 cups Butterfinger candy. Top cooled bars with frosting. Refrigerate at least 2 hours before slicing and serving.

FAMILY FAVORITES

MIX AND MATCH IDEAS

MAKING MEALS, MAKING MEMORIES

The best part of my day is sitting around the table and breaking bread with the people I love. Whether that's a regular old Tuesday night with my husband and three kids, a huge holiday fete with twinkle lights and Christmas music, or a patio supper overlooking the pool while we wear wet swimsuits and have bare feet, it's the people and the love that matter most. Dinner should be a time of fellowship, a time of honesty, a time of sharing our highs and lows from the day, with lots of laughing and easy conversation. The table is where we come back to each and every night...so my goal is to have a meal on it but the focus is on the people I love.

Post your dinner pics, I'm listening.
#mixandmatchmeals

INDEX OF RECIPES

SHAY SHULL

is the author of the *Mix and Match Mama* blog. Daily, she writes about motherhood, adoption, world travel, holidays, organization, and, of course, yummy food.

Passionate about coffee, traveling the world with her family, and Red Sox baseball, her greatest love is Christ. Shay lives in McKinney, Texas, with her husband, Andrew, and their three kids, Kensington, Smith, and Ashby.

Follow Shay on social media as @MixandMatchMama.

WANT MORE SWEET IDEAS FROM SHAY?

Mix-and-Match Cakes is the icing on top of all the amazing meals you'll be making. Shay will show you 101 mouthwatering Bundt cakes by using her simple mix-and-match method. It will change your family's dinner table conversation from "Can I be excused now?" to "Wow!" Now available wherever books are sold.

To learn more about Harvest House books and
to read sample chapters, visit our website:

www.harvesthousepublishers.com

HARVEST HOUSE PUBLISHERS
EUGENE, OREGON